RHODESIAN BUSH WAR

DECOLONIZATION, CONFLICT, AND NATIONHOOD IN SOUTHERN AFRICA

DANIEL WRINN

CONTENTS

GET YOUR FREE COPY OF WW2: SPIES, SNIPERS AND THE WORLD AT WAR

Never miss a new release by signing up for my free readers group. You'll also get WW2: Spies, Snipers and Tales of the World at War delivered to your inbox. (You can unsubscribe at any time.) Go to wrinnmilitaryhistory.com to join.

INTRODUCTION

The Rhodesian Bush War, also known as the Second Chimurenga, was a guerrilla conflict that unfolded between 1964 and 1979, marking a significant and bloody chapter in Southern Africa's history. At its core, the war pitted the white minority government of Rhodesia, led by Prime Minister Ian Smith, against two African nationalist movements—ZANU (Zimbabwe African National Union) and ZAPU (Zimbabwe African People's Union)—both fighting for the end of white minority rule and the establishment of majority-led governance. This conflict didn't occur in isolation, but was deeply intertwined with the broader Cold War context, as well as the global wave of decolonization sweeping across Africa. The war ultimately culminated in the establishment of the independent state of Zimbabwe in 1980.

However, to understand the significance of the Rhodesian Bush War, we must first consider the complex dynamics that led to this long and violent struggle. At its heart, the war was about the future of a country and its people—those who had long called Rhodesia home, both descendants of white *settlers and black Africans.

*From this point onward, the terms "settlers" and "white settlers" will refer to both the original Europeans who colonized Rhodesia and their descendants. These descendants were born and raised in Rhodesia, knowing no other home than Africa.

The white settlers, often vilified in mainstream historical accounts, believed they were defending their homes, livelihoods, and the stability of a nation they had helped build through hard work and determination. From their perspective, the rise of African nationalism posed not just a political challenge, but an existential threat to the way of life they had forged in Rhodesia.

White settlers in Rhodesia were a small but highly influential minority who held political and economic power. Many of them traced their roots back to European colonization, particularly British settlement efforts in the late nineteenth and early twentieth centuries. By the mid-twentieth century, Rhodesia had developed into a thriving, albeit segregated, society with a strong economy rooted in agriculture, mining, and industry. For many of these settlers and their families, Rhodesia was home. They had invested generations of labor into the land, building farms, businesses, and infrastructure. Thus, when African nationalist movements began demanding majority rule, many white Rhodesians saw this as a direct threat to their way of life, not simply in terms of political power, but in the form of potential land confiscations, economic collapse, and violence.

In 1965, Ian Smith's Rhodesian Front government

took the drastic step of issuing a Unilateral Declaration of Independence (UDI) from Britain. This bold move was, in part, a response to growing pressure from the British government to implement majority rule, something that white Rhodesians feared would lead to the kind of instability and violence that had been seen in other newly independent African nations. Smith, a veteran of World War II and a staunch defender of white Rhodesian interests, believed that the country was better off under continued white leadership. He argued that immediate majority rule would result in chaos, given the lack of political experience and infrastructure among the black African majority.

It is crucial to understand that many white settlers viewed themselves as defenders of Rhodesia's stability and prosperity. They believed that they were not simply fighting to maintain political control but were also protecting the nation from the potential economic and social collapse that could come with a sudden transition to majority rule. From their perspective, the war was about ensuring the future of a country that had thrived under their governance and hard work.

On the other side of the conflict were the African nationalist movements, primarily ZANU and ZAPU, which represented the aspirations of the black majority. These movements were not monolithic; ZANU, led by Robert Mugabe, followed a Marxist-Maoist ideology and sought support from China, while ZAPU, under Joshua Nkomo, aligned more closely with the Soviet Union and adopted a more traditional Marxist approach. Both movements were committed to ending white minority rule, but they differed in their strategies and visions for post-independence Rhodesia.

The African nationalist forces, particularly ZANLA (ZANU's military wing) and ZIPRA (ZAPU's military wing), operated as guerrilla armies, launching attacks on white Rhodesian targets and infrastructure. The nationalist forces relied on tactics that were unconventional, focusing on rural areas and targeting both military and civilian installations. These tactics created a climate of fear and insecurity among white Rhodesians, who were already deeply concerned about the potential for a violent revolution.

From the settlers' point of view, the African nationalist movements were often seen not as liberators, but as violent insurgents who posed a grave threat to the safety of all Rhodesians. Guerrilla attacks, often indiscriminate in nature, targeted farms, schools, and even churches. Families living in remote areas were especially vulnerable, and many white settlers took up arms, joining paramilitary forces or local defense units to protect their homes and communities. For these settlers, the war was not just about maintaining political control but about defending their very lives against what they saw as terrorist attacks.

The global context of the Cold War further complicated the Rhodesian Bush War. Both sides of the conflict were backed by foreign powers. While the African nationalist movements received military and financial support from China, the Soviet Union, and neighboring African countries like Mozambique and Zambia, Rhodesia found itself increasingly isolated on the international stage. The United Nations imposed sanctions on Rhodesia following the UDI, and the British government refused to recognize the Smith administration. Despite this, Rhodesia managed to survive for over a decade, relying on clandestine trade with sympathetic nations and its strong military capabilities.

Rhodesia's military forces, including the elite Selous Scouts and the Rhodesian Light Infantry, became known for their effectiveness in counter-insurgency operations. These units carried out daring raids into neighboring countries where guerrilla forces were based and utilized advanced counter-guerrilla tactics to combat the insurgency. Yet, despite these military successes, Rhodesia faced increasing pressure both domestically and internationally. The war had taken a toll on the country's economy, and morale among the white population began to erode as the conflict dragged on without a clear end in sight.

By the late 1970s, it became clear that the war could not be won militarily. Both sides were exhausted, and international pressure for a negotiated settlement grew. In 1979, after years of conflict, the Lancaster House Agreement was reached, bringing an end to the war and paving the way for majority rule. The following year, Zimbabwe was born, with Robert Mugabe as its first Prime Minister.

In hindsight, the Rhodesian Bush War is often portrayed as a straightforward struggle between oppressed African nationalists and an oppressive white minority government. The reality is far more complex. While African nationalist forces fought for their right to self-determination, many white Rhodesians genuinely believed they were defending themselves against violent insurgents and the potential collapse of their country. For them, the war was not about clinging to power for its own sake, but about protecting a way of life that they had worked hard to build.

As we explore this conflict, we will delve into the key events, battles, and strategies that shaped the course of the war, examining both sides of the struggle and offering a balanced view of one of Africa's most significant and controversial conflicts.

COLONIALISM AND MINORITY RULE

To understand the roots of the Rhodesian Bush War, it is essential to examine the colonial history of Rhodesia and the socio-political dynamics that led to the conflict. This history is deeply tied to British imperialism, economic interests, and the eventual rise of white settler dominance, particularly under the leadership of figures like Cecil Rhodes. Rhodesia, named after Cecil Rhodes, was established as part of the British South Africa Company's expansion into Southern Africa, and from the outset, it was designed to serve the economic interests of British settlers and colonial powers.

The roots of white minority rule in Rhodesia can be traced back to the late nineteenth century when Cecil Rhodes, a British businessman and imperialist, sought to expand British influence in Africa. Through the British South Africa Company, Rhodes secured land from local African leaders—often under questionable terms—and established what would become Southern Rhodesia in 1923. This was part of a broader British imperial strategy to secure raw materials, agricultural land, and geopolitical dominance in the region.

From its inception, Rhodesia was built on a system of segregation that favored the white settler minority. While many of these settlers were hardworking farmers, ranchers, and entrepreneurs, the colonial system ensured that they had access to the best land, political power, and economic resources. African communities, on the other hand, were marginalized, their land was often confiscated, and they were relegated to low-wage labor roles in the agricultural and mining sectors. The colonial government enacted laws that restricted African political participation and limited their economic opportunities, creating deep social and economic inequalities.

White settlers, primarily of British descent, viewed themselves as the rightful stewards of Rhodesia's land and resources. They believed that their governance, industry, and agricultural prowess were essential for maintaining order and prosperity. Many settlers felt entitled to the land, believing that they had "tamed" a wild and undeveloped region, turning it into a successful colony. To them, the growing calls for African majority rule posed an existential threat—not just to their political control, but to the economic and social stability they had built over decades.

While the British government initially supported white minority rule in Rhodesia, the winds of change were beginning to blow across Africa by the mid-twentieth century. After World War II, the global tide of decolonization gained momentum. The United Kingdom, facing economic hardships and pressure from both the United Nations and emerging African leaders, began to distance itself from its imperial past. Britain started pushing for political reforms in its African colonies, advocating for majority rule and the end of colonialism. This push created friction between the British government and the white settler leadership in Rhodesia, which was determined to hold onto power.

As Britain moved toward decolonization, white settlers in Rhodesia sought to solidify their hold on the country. By the early 1960s, many African countries were gaining independence, and white minority regimes in Africa were becoming increasingly isolated. In Rhodesia, the white population—although small in number—held the vast majority of wealth, land, and political power due to deliberate policies that had been in place since the colony's inception.

White Rhodesians, like their counterparts in South Africa, believed in the necessity of segregation and minority rule to maintain what they saw as the country's stability and success. They argued that the black African population was not yet ready for self-governance and that majority rule would lead to chaos, economic decline, and violence. The settlers pointed to the post-independence struggles of other African nations, where new governments often faced civil unrest, economic challenges, and coups. This view was reinforced by their own experiences, as many settlers had invested generations of labor into the land and economy, building a prosperous and functioning society.

It is important to acknowledge that white settlers were not a monolithic group. While some, particularly the political elites, advocated for maintaining absolute control, others supported gradual reforms or greater political inclusion for Africans. However, the general consensus among white Rhodesians was that immediate majority rule would be disastrous for the country.

In 1965, this belief culminated in the Unilateral Declaration of Independence (UDI) by Ian Smith's government. Smith, a World War II veteran and leader of the Rhodesian Front, became Prime Minister in 1964. He was a staunch advocate for maintaining white minority rule and believed that Rhodesia could survive as an independent nation without the oversight of Britain or the influence of African nationalist movements. The UDI was a bold and unprecedented move, making Rhodesia the first British colony to unilaterally declare independence without seeking approval from the Crown.

Smith's decision to declare independence was driven by several factors. First, there was a growing belief among white Rhodesians that Britain had abandoned them. The British government's insistence on transitioning to majority rule was seen as a betrayal of the white settlers who had built Rhodesia into a successful and prosperous country. Second, the white population feared the rising tide of African nationalism. Movements like ZANU and ZAPU were gaining strength, supported by external powers such as China and the Soviet Union. Many white Rhodesians viewed these groups not as freedom fighters but as communist-inspired insurgents who sought to overthrow the established order through violence.

Smith's government framed the UDI as an act of self-defense, necessary to protect Rhodesia from the chaos that had engulfed other African nations following decolonization. The settler leadership argued that immediate majority rule would lead to the destruction of Rhodesia's economy, social fabric, and way of life. Smith famously declared that there would be "no majority rule in Rhodesia, not in a thousand years," reflecting the determination of the white government to hold onto power at any cost.

The UDI, however, isolated Rhodesia internationally. The British government, under Prime Minister Harold Wilson, refused to recognize the Smith regime and imposed economic sanctions on Rhodesia. The United Nations followed suit, and Rhodesia became a pariah state, with few international allies. South Africa and Portugal were among the few countries that provided support to Rhodesia, but even this was limited due to the increasing pressure from the international community.

The UDI did not bring the stability that Smith and the white Rhodesian government had hoped for. Instead, it set the stage for a prolonged and bloody conflict between the white minority government and African nationalist forces. The sanctions crippled Rhodesia's economy, while guerrilla forces from ZANU and ZAPU began launching attacks on white farms, infrastructure, and government forces. These attacks, combined with the international isolation of Rhodesia, created a climate of fear and uncertainty among the white population.

While the white settlers saw themselves as defending their homes and way of life, the African majority viewed the UDI as an illegal act of defiance that further entrenched an oppressive and unjust system. This clash of perspectives fueled the violence that would define the next fifteen years of Rhodesian history, as both sides fought for the future of the country.

THE RISE OF NATIONALIST MOVEMENTS: ZANU AND ZAPU

THE RISE OF AFRICAN NATIONALIST MOVEMENTS IN Rhodesia was a direct response to the rigid structure of white minority rule that emerged from the colonial era. Two of the most prominent and influential groups that rose to challenge the Rhodesian government were the Zimbabwe African National Union (ZANU) and the Zimbabwe African People's Union (ZAPU). Both organizations played a central role in the guerrilla war that would shape the future of Rhodesia, but they were far from united. ZANU and ZAPU had distinct ideological differences, tactical approaches, and international alliances that influenced their respective strategies throughout the conflict.

The roots of ZANU and ZAPU lie in the broader Pan-Africanist movements that emerged across the African continent during the mid-twentieth century. These movements sought to end colonial rule and establish independent African states. In Rhodesia, African nationalists were inspired by the successes of neighboring countries such as Zambia and Mozambique, which had successfully ousted colonial powers and established majority rule. The growing sentiment among black Africans in Rhodesia was that white minority rule was not only unjust but unsustainable in the face of the global decolonization wave.

However, despite their shared goal of overthrowing the Rhodesian government and establishing black majority rule, ZANU and ZAPU were divided along ideological lines.

ZAPU, founded in 1961 and led by Joshua Nkomo, was the first significant African nationalist organization to emerge in Rhodesia. ZAPU's ideology was rooted in a Marxist-Leninist framework, which emphasized class struggle, the redistribution of wealth, and state control of the economy. Nkomo, who had a more pragmatic approach, sought to build a broad coalition that included different ethnic groups and classes. His vision was for a united Zimbabwe that would transcend ethnic divisions, although ZAPU had a strong base of support among the Ndebele people, one of the two major ethnic groups in Rhodesia.

ZAPU's military wing, the Zimbabwe People's Revolutionary Army (ZIPRA), was structured along Soviet lines, with a focus on conventional military tactics, including preparing for large-scale engagements and establishing a standing army. Nkomo and his allies sought assistance from the Soviet Union, which provided training, weapons, and financial support. ZAPU's strategy was shaped by its Soviet backing, which emphasized the importance of political education and building a professional military force capable of confronting Rhodesian forces directly.

On the other hand, ZANU, which broke away from

ZAPU in 1963, was led by Robert Mugabe after internal power struggles. ZANU's ideological approach was heavily influenced by Maoism, a branch of Marxism that emphasized the role of rural peasants in revolution. Mugabe and ZANU believed that the path to victory lay in mobilizing the rural population to engage in guerrilla warfare, harassing Rhodesian forces through hit-and-run tactics and gradually wearing them down. ZANU's military wing, the Zimbabwe African National Liberation Army (ZANLA), embraced these tactics, which had been employed successfully by communist insurgencies in China and Vietnam.

Mugabe and his supporters advocated for a more radical approach than Nkomo, believing that the rural peasantry, rather than urban workers or political elites, would be the key to achieving revolution. ZANU's Maoist ideology placed a heavy emphasis on land reform and the redistribution of farmland, which resonated with the grievances of black Rhodesian farmers who had been dispossessed of their land by white settlers.

One of the most significant factors influencing the trajectory of the Rhodesian Bush War was the international support received by ZANU and ZAPU. Both groups were able to draw on support from powerful communist nations, particularly China and the Soviet Union, which saw the Rhodesian conflict as part of the broader struggle against Western imperialism during the Cold War.

ZANU established close ties with the People's Republic of China, which was eager to spread its revolutionary ideology across the African continent. Chinese military advisors provided ZANLA with training in guerrilla warfare, and large shipments of Chinese-made weapons were sent to support the insurgency. ZANLA fighters were trained in Maoist guerrilla tactics, which involved using the terrain to their advantage, launching ambushes, and avoiding direct confrontations with better-armed Rhodesian forces. The Chinese influence on ZANU's strategy was unmistakable; Mugabe and other ZANU leaders often spoke in terms of a "protracted people's war," echoing the language of Maoist revolutionary doctrine.

China's support was not only ideological but also practical. The Chinese Communist Party saw Rhodesia as a potential foothold for its influence in Southern Africa, which was strategically important given its proximity to South Africa, another flashpoint in the global struggle against white minority rule. Chinese aid to ZANU allowed the movement to expand its operations, particularly in the eastern regions of Rhodesia, where the guerrillas were able to establish a strong presence among rural communities.

ZAPU, by contrast, maintained a closer relationship with the Soviet Union. The Soviets, wary of China's growing influence in Africa, sought to counterbalance Chinese support for ZANU by backing ZAPU. ZIPRA fighters (Zimbabwe People's Revolutionary Army) were trained in the Soviet Union and Eastern Bloc countries, and they received Soviet-made arms and equipment. Unlike ZANLA, which focused on guerrilla warfare, ZIPRA's military strategy was more conventional, with an emphasis on preparing for a direct confrontation with the Rhodesian army. ZIPRA even established a semi-professional standing army based in Zambia, from which it launched cross-border raids into Rhodesia.

ZAPU's relationship with the Soviet Union shaped its political ideology as well. While Nkomo did not advocate for the same level of radical land reform as Mugabe, he envisioned a future Zimbabwe in which the state would control key industries and resources, in line with the Soviet model of centralized economic planning. Nkomo's approach was seen as more moderate by some, but it also alienated certain factions within the nationalist movement who were impatient for more immediate and radical change.

The split between ZANU and ZAPU was not just ideological; it was also deeply personal. Mugabe and Nkomo were rivals, and their mutual distrust prevented the two groups from effectively coordinating their efforts against the Rhodesian government. This division would have significant consequences for the course of the war, as it allowed the Rhodesian government to exploit the internal rivalries within the nationalist movement. The lack of unity between ZANU and ZAPU also weakened the African nationalist cause, as both groups vied for supremacy rather than focusing solely on defeating the white minority regime.

In addition to support from China and the Soviet Union, both ZANU and ZAPU received assistance from neighboring African countries, particularly Mozambique and Zambia. These countries, having recently won their own struggles for independence, were sympathetic to the African nationalist movements in Rhodesia and allowed ZANU and ZAPU to establish bases on their territory. Mozambique, in particular, became a crucial staging ground for ZANLA operations after the country gained independence from Portugal in 1975.

The division between ZANU and ZAPU had a profound impact on the course of the guerrilla war. Rather than presenting a united front, the two movements often operated independently, each focusing on different regions and employing different tactics. ZANLA fighters, operating primarily in the eastern part of the country, relied on their guerrilla tactics to carry out ambushes and sabotage missions. ZIPRA, on the other hand, concentrated its efforts in the west, launching more conventional military operations from its bases in Zambia.

This lack of coordination between the two groups gave the Rhodesian government a strategic advantage. Ian Smith's government, although outnumbered, was able to mount a more effective defense against the insurgency by exploiting the rivalry between ZANU and ZAPU. Rhodesian forces, including elite units like the Selous Scouts, employed counter-insurgency tactics designed to disrupt the guerrilla networks and prevent them from gaining a foothold in the rural areas.

However, despite their differences and occasional infighting, ZANU and ZAPU were united in their ultimate goal of toppling the Rhodesian government and ending white minority rule. Their ability to sustain a long-running guerrilla war, despite internal divisions and limited resources, was a testament to the depth of the grievances of the black African majority that had fueled the nationalist movements.

As the conflict dragged on into the late 1970s, it became increasingly clear that neither side could achieve a decisive victory on the battlefield. International pressure on Rhodesia mounted, and the white minority government found itself increasingly isolated. Meanwhile, the nationalist movements, bolstered by their external support, continued to escalate their attacks, leading to a growing sense of urgency for a negotiated settlement.

ESCALATION OF THE GUERRILLA WAR

The early 1970s marked a significant turning point in the Rhodesian Bush War. As ZANU and ZAPU intensified their guerrilla campaigns, the conflict entered a more violent and chaotic phase. Between 1972 and 1976, the war escalated as the guerrilla forces of ZANLA (ZANU's military wing) and ZIPRA (ZAPU's military wing) launched more sophisticated and coordinated attacks against the Rhodesian government. This period also saw the Rhodesian military implement a range of counter-insurgency strategies to combat the growing insurgency, most notably the formation of the elite Selous Scouts.

Two of the key early events that marked the beginning of this intensified phase of the guerrilla war were the Wankie and Sipolilo campaigns (1972–1973). These campaigns were major efforts by ZIPRA and ZANLA forces to infiltrate Rhodesia from neighboring countries and establish a presence in the country's rural areas.

The Wankie Campaign saw ZIPRA forces attempting to cross from Zambia into western Rhodesia with the goal of linking up with South African insurgents from the African National Congress (ANC). This was part of a broader strategy to spread the guerrilla war into South Africa, thereby expanding the conflict and putting additional pressure on the Rhodesian government.

The Wankie Campaign ultimately ended in failure for ZIPRA. Despite early successes, the Rhodesian Security Forces, employing their superior knowledge of the terrain and effective counter-insurgency tactics, were able to track down and eliminate most of the ZIPRA fighters involved in the operation. The Selous Scouts, an elite Rhodesian special forces unit formed specifically for counter-insurgency operations, played a pivotal role in disrupting ZIPRA's movements. The Selous Scouts specialized in infiltrating guerrilla groups and carrying out reconnaissance missions deep behind enemy lines. They were notorious for their ruthless efficiency, often using the same guerrilla tactics as their opponents to outmaneuver and neutralize insurgent forces.

The failure of the Wankie and Sipolilo campaigns underscored the difficulties faced by the guerrilla forces in trying to establish a foothold in Rhodesia's rural areas. However, these operations also marked a turning point in the war. For the first time, ZANLA and ZIPRA were able to demonstrate their ability to coordinate large-scale military operations, and the Rhodesian government began to realize that the insurgency was evolving into a more formidable threat. While the early campaigns may not have succeeded in achieving their immediate objectives, they did help to shift the momentum of the war in favor of the nationalist forces by highlighting the vulnerabilities of the Rhodesian regime.

As the war progressed, ZANLA and ZIPRA refined their strategies, adapting their tactics to better exploit the weaknesses of the Rhodesian military. ZANLA, under Robert Mugabe's leadership, continued to focus on Maoist-inspired guerrilla warfare. ZANLA's strategy was built around the principle of "people's war," which sought to mobilize the rural population as both a support base and a resource for recruitment. ZANLA fighters would move into rural areas, often targeting isolated white-owned farms or police outposts, and attempt to win the support of local villagers through a combination of propaganda and intimidation. This strategy allowed ZANLA to build up a network of informants and supply lines that could sustain their operations over long periods.

One of the key tactics employed by ZANLA was ambush warfare. ZANLA fighters, using the dense bush and rugged terrain to their advantage, would lay ambushes along key transportation routes, targeting Rhodesian military convoys, supply trucks, and civilian vehicles. These ambushes were designed to inflict maximum casualties and disrupt the Rhodesian government's ability to maintain control over rural areas. The ambushes also had a psychological effect, as they spread fear and insecurity among both the white settlers and black Africans who collaborated with the Rhodesian government.

ZIPRA, led by Joshua Nkomo, took a different approach. Rather than relying solely on guerrilla tactics, ZIPRA began to prepare for more conventional military operations. With significant support from the Soviet

Union, ZIPRA was able to build a more structured and professional fighting force, complete with heavy weaponry, including armored vehicles and anti-aircraft guns. ZIPRA's long-term strategy was to engage in large-scale battles with Rhodesian forces, with the ultimate goal of seizing control of key urban centers. However, ZIPRA's reliance on conventional tactics proved to be a double-edged sword. While it allowed ZIPRA to challenge the Rhodesian military more directly, it also made ZIPRA forces more vulnerable to airstrikes and counter-attacks.

One of the most significant developments during this period was the growing role of neighboring countries in the conflict. Mozambique, which gained independence from Portugal in 1975, became a key ally of ZANLA. With the fall of the Portuguese colonial government, ZANLA was able to establish bases inside Mozambique, from which it launched cross-border attacks into Rhodesia. This gave ZANLA a strategic advantage, as it allowed them to operate from a safe haven just across the border, making it more difficult for the Rhodesian military to contain the insurgency.

At the same time, Zambia continued to provide support for ZIPRA, allowing them to operate from bases within Zambian territory. This cross-border element of the war posed a significant challenge for the Rhodesian government, as it forced them to extend their military operations into neighboring countries. The Rhodesian military frequently conducted air raids and ground assaults on guerrilla camps in Mozambique and Zambia, but these operations often led to diplomatic tensions and international condemnation, further isolating the Rhodesian regime on the global stage.

In response to the escalating insurgency, the Rhodesian government developed a comprehensive counter-insurgency strategy that combined conventional military tactics with psychological warfare and political repression. One of the key elements of this strategy was the formation of the Selous Scouts. This elite unit, named after the famous British explorer and hunter Frederick Selous, was tasked with carrying out covert operations against the guerrilla forces. The Selous Scouts became infamous for their use of deception and infiltration tactics, often disguising themselves as guerrilla fighters to gather intelligence and carry out assassinations behind enemy lines.

The Selous Scouts were highly effective at disrupting guerrilla operations. Their ability to blend in with the local population and their deep knowledge of the terrain allowed them to track down and eliminate guerrilla leaders with remarkable precision. In addition to their covert operations, the Rhodesian military also relied heavily on air power to target guerrilla bases in remote areas. Rhodesian fighter jets and helicopters were used to carry out bombing raids on suspected guerrilla camps, often causing significant casualties among both fighters and civilians.

However, despite their military successes, the Rhodesian counter-insurgency efforts were not without controversy. The brutality of the Rhodesian forces, particularly the use of torture, summary executions, and collective punishment, alienated large segments of the black population. The Rhodesian government's reliance on repressive measures, such as the establishment of protected villages (which were essentially internment camps for rural Africans), only served to increase support for the guerrilla movements. Many black Rhodesians saw the government's actions as further evidence of the regime's illegitimacy, and this helped to swell the ranks of ZANLA and ZIPRA.

The white settler population in Rhodesia also played a key role in the counter-insurgency efforts. Many white farmers, particularly those living in remote areas, took up arms to defend their properties from guerrilla attacks. These farmers were often members of the Rhodesian Light Infantry or local defense units, which worked closely with the Rhodesian military to patrol rural areas and respond to guerrilla incursions. For many white Rhodesians, the war was not just a political struggle but a fight for survival. The guerrilla attacks on white-owned farms, combined with the government's propaganda efforts, fostered a siege mentality among the white population. Many settlers believed that they were defending their homes and livelihoods from a foreign-backed communist insurgency.

Despite their superior firepower and tactical advantages, the Rhodesian forces were unable to completely suppress the guerrilla war. The insurgency continued to grow, fueled by the grievances of the black majority and the support of external powers. By 1976, it was clear that the war was entering a new phase, one in which neither side could achieve a decisive military victory. The Rhodesian government, facing increasing isolation and economic hardship, began to explore the possibility of a negotiated settlement.

INTERNATIONAL INVOLVEMENT
AND THE GLOBAL STAGE

The Rhodesian Bush War was not only a conflict within the borders of Rhodesia; it was deeply intertwined with the global dynamics of the Cold War and the decolonization of Africa. International involvement played a significant role in shaping the course of the war, with the guerrilla movements receiving support from communist powers like the Soviet Union and China, while Rhodesia found backing from its white minority neighbors, especially apartheid South Africa and Portuguese-controlled Mozambique. The international dimension of the Rhodesian Bush War was deeply influenced by Cold War rivalries, economic sanctions, and diplomatic efforts, which shaped the trajectory of the conflict and its eventual resolution.

This conflict unfolded against the backdrop of the Cold War, a period of global tension between the capitalist West, led by the United States and its allies, and the communist bloc, dominated by the Soviet Union and China. The conflict in Rhodesia, much like other regional struggles in Africa, Latin America, and Asia, became a proxy battleground for these superpowers.

The African nationalist movements in Rhodesia, particularly ZANU and ZAPU, aligned themselves with the communist powers. Both movements received significant military, financial, and ideological support from the Soviet Union, China, and their allies. This support was part of a broader strategy by the communist bloc to gain influence in Africa by backing revolutionary movements that sought to overthrow colonial or white minority governments. In the eyes of the Soviet Union and China, the Rhodesian Bush War was not just about African independence but about expanding communist influence in a region dominated by Western capitalist powers.

ZANU, under the leadership of Robert Mugabe, established close ties with the People's Republic of China. Chinese support for ZANU was rooted in Maoist revolutionary doctrine, which emphasized the role of rural peasants in guerrilla warfare and revolution. Chinese military advisors provided ZANLA, ZANU's military wing, with training in guerrilla tactics, while large shipments of Chinese-made weapons, including AK-47 rifles and rocket-propelled grenades, were sent to support the insurgency. China saw Rhodesia as a key battleground in its efforts to spread Maoist ideology in Africa and counter the influence of both Western capitalism and Soviet-style communism.

On the other hand, ZAPU, led by Joshua Nkomo, leaned toward the Soviet Union for support. The Soviet Union, wary of Chinese influence in Southern Africa, backed ZAPU as part of its broader strategy to gain a foothold in the region. The Soviet Union provided

ZIPRA, ZAPU's military wing, with extensive military training, weapons, and financial assistance. Unlike ZANLA, which focused on guerrilla warfare, ZIPRA's strategy was more conventional, with Soviet advisors helping to build a semi-professional army capable of engaging in large-scale battles with Rhodesian forces.

This international backing from communist powers allowed the guerrilla movements to sustain their campaigns against the Rhodesian government. However, the Cold War dynamics also complicated the nationalist struggle. The rivalry between China and the Soviet Union contributed to the split between ZANU and ZAPU, with each group aligning itself with a different superpower. This division weakened the overall effectiveness of the nationalist forces, as ZANU and ZAPU often competed for resources and influence rather than presenting a united front against the Rhodesian government.

Rhodesia, under the leadership of Ian Smith, found itself increasingly isolated on the international stage following its Unilateral Declaration of Independence (UDI) in 1965. The UDI declared Rhodesia's independence from Britain while maintaining white minority rule. The United Nations, led by Britain, imposed economic sanctions on Rhodesia in an attempt to force the Smith government to implement majority rule. These sanctions included bans on trade, arms sales, and the export of Rhodesian goods such as tobacco and minerals.

While the sanctions had a significant impact on Rhodesia's economy, they did not immediately bring about the desired political change. Rhodesia, although isolated, managed to survive for more than a decade after the UDI by finding ways to circumvent the sanctions. The Rhodesian government relied on clandestine trade networks, smuggling, and the support of sympathetic countries to maintain its economy and military capabilities. South Africa and Portugal, both of which had their own vested interests in preserving white minority rule in Southern Africa, were key allies in helping Rhodesia evade the sanctions.

However, the international isolation of Rhodesia had other consequences. The sanctions created a siege mentality among the white settler population, reinforcing their belief that they were defending their country not only from African nationalists but from a global conspiracy aimed at destroying their way of life. This sense of isolation also fueled the determination of the Rhodesian government and military to resist majority rule at all costs, leading to a hardening of positions and a reluctance to negotiate.

Despite its resilience, Rhodesia could not escape the long-term effects of international sanctions. By the mid-1970s, the country's economy was in decline, with shortages of essential goods, rising inflation, and a shrinking tax base. The sanctions, combined with the escalating costs of the guerrilla war, placed an unsustainable burden on the Rhodesian government. While Rhodesia's military continued to perform well on the battlefield, the economic strain and international pressure for a political settlement became increasingly difficult to ignore.

One of Rhodesia's most important allies during the Bush War was South Africa, which shared a common interest in maintaining white minority rule in the region. South Africa, under its apartheid regime, viewed

Rhodesia as a buffer state against the spread of African nationalism and communism. The fall of Rhodesia to nationalist forces would have been seen as a direct threat to the stability of South Africa, which faced its own insurgency from the African National Congress (ANC).

South Africa provided Rhodesia with critical military and economic support throughout the war, including troops and weapons such as the Belgian FN FAL rifle, claymore mines, and aircraft. South African troops were deployed to assist Rhodesian forces in key battles, particularly along the border with Mozambique, where ZANLA guerrillas operated. South Africa also supplied Rhodesia with fuel, weapons, and other essential goods, helping the country to survive the effects of international sanctions.

South Africa's support for Rhodesia was not unconditional. By the late 1970s, it became clear that the guerrilla war was not going to be won militarily, and South Africa began to push for a negotiated settlement. The apartheid regime, facing increasing international pressure and its own internal challenges, could no longer afford to prop up Rhodesia indefinitely. South Africa's decision to withdraw its military support in the late 1970s left Rhodesia even more vulnerable to the insurgency.

Portugal, which controlled Mozambique and Angola, also played a key role in supporting Rhodesia, particularly in the early stages of the war. Mozambique was strategically important to Rhodesia, as it provided access to the sea and served as a buffer against ZANLA guerrilla forces. However, the situation changed dramatically in 1975 when Portugal's colonial empire collapsed following the Carnation Revolution. The independence of Mozambique, which quickly aligned itself with the Soviet Union and China, allowed ZANLA to establish bases on Rhodesia's eastern border, from which it could launch cross-border attacks. The loss of Portuguese support was a significant blow to the white Rhodesians, as it allowed the guerrilla movements to intensify their operations and increased the pressure on the Rhodesian government.

Throughout the Rhodesian Bush War, various diplomatic efforts were made to bring about a peaceful settlement to the conflict. Britain, as the former colonial power, played a central role in these efforts, although its influence over the Smith government was limited after the UDI. British governments, both Labor and Conservative, consistently sought a negotiated solution that would lead to majority rule while preserving the economic and political interests of the white minority.

Several attempts were made to mediate between the Rhodesian government and the nationalist movements, but these efforts were repeatedly undermined by a lack of trust and the uncompromising positions of both sides. Ian Smith, despite facing growing pressure, was reluctant to make meaningful concessions, fearing that majority rule would lead to the destruction of Rhodesia's economy and the displacement of the white population. On the other hand, the nationalist movements, buoyed by their international support and years of suppression, were unwilling to settle for anything less than full independence and majority rule.

One of the most significant diplomatic efforts was the Geneva Conference of 1976, which brought together representatives from the Rhodesian government, ZANU, ZAPU, and other African leaders in an attempt to negotiate a settlement. The conference, however, ended in failure, as the parties were unable to agree on the terms of a transitional government. The failure of the Geneva Conference highlighted the deep divisions between the nationalist movements and the Rhodesian government, as well as the limitations of British mediation.

The war was part of a broader struggle for influence in Africa during a period of intense global rivalry between the capitalist West and the communist bloc. Ultimately, the combination of international pressure and the escalating insurgency would force the Rhodesian government to seek a political solution, setting the stage for the eventual transition to majority rule and the creation of Zimbabwe in 1980.

OPERATION DINGO AND THE CLOSING YEARS

As the Rhodesian Bush War dragged into its final years, the intensity of the conflict reached new heights. Both sides—white minority rule under Ian Smith's Rhodesian government and the African nationalist guerrilla forces—were entrenched in a bitter struggle full of minefields, the killing of women and children on both sides, and chemical weapons use, with neither able to secure a decisive victory. The tragic military operations, significant political shifts, and mounting external pressures ultimately forced the Rhodesian government to enter negotiations, leading to the transition from Rhodesia to the newly independent state of Zimbabwe in 1980.

One of the most significant military operations of the closing years of the war was Operation Dingo, which took place in late 1977. This large scale offensive was aimed at crippling the Zimbabwe African National Liberation Army (ZANLA), ZANU's military wing, by launching a surprise attack on its bases in Mozambique. These bases, located in Chimoio and Tembue, had become major training grounds for ZANLA fighters, and their proximity to Rhodesia's border posed an increasing threat to the Rhodesian government.

The Rhodesian military planned Operation Dingo with meticulous detail. The operation involved a combination of air strikes, paratrooper assaults, and ground forces, and it was one of the most audacious military operations of the war. On November 23, 1977, the Rhodesian Air Force launched a series of air raids on ZANLA's Chimoio base, catching the guerrillas by surprise. This was followed by an airborne assault, with paratroopers and elite special forces being deployed to mop up any remaining resistance.

Operation Dingo was a tactical success for the Rhodesian forces. It resulted in the deaths of several thousand ZANLA fighters and destroyed significant amounts of equipment, infrastructure, and supplies. The operation temporarily weakened ZANLA's ability to conduct guerrilla operations within Rhodesia, and for a short time, it seemed as though the Rhodesian government had dealt a crippling blow to the nationalist forces.

However, the long-term strategic impact of Operation Dingo was far more complicated. While the Rhodesians succeeded in disrupting ZANLA's operations in Mozambique, they failed to achieve a decisive victory that could turn the tide of the war. ZANLA's leadership, including Robert Mugabe, remained intact, and the organization quickly rebuilt its forces with the help of its allies in Mozambique, China, and the Soviet Union. In fact, the operation had an unintended consequence: it galvanized ZANLA's resolve to continue the fight and attracted even more recruits to their cause. Operation Dingo demonstrated that while Rhodesia had a highly capable military, it could not permanently eliminate the guerrilla threat.

By the late 1970s, international sanctions were beginning to have a more severe impact on Rhodesia's economy and ability to wage war. The country was increasingly isolated on the global stage, with very few allies left to support its white minority government. South Africa, its most important ally, was itself facing growing internal and external pressures due to its apartheid policies and had started to distance itself from the Rhodesian cause. South African leader John Vorster, recognizing that Rhodesia was becoming a liability, pressured Ian Smith to consider negotiations with the nationalist movements.

The military stalemate between Rhodesian forces and the nationalist guerrillas further compounded the government's problems. Despite their superior training and equipment, Rhodesian forces could not decisively defeat ZANLA or ZIPRA. Guerrilla warfare, by its nature, is difficult to combat with conventional military strategies, and the Rhodesians found themselves locked in a cycle of ambushes, raids, and counter-attacks that sapped both morale and resources. The sheer number of guerrilla fighters, combined with their ability to blend into the rural population and launch surprise attacks, made it impossible for Rhodesian forces to gain the upper hand in the conflict.

As the war dragged on, internal pressure also began to build within Rhodesia. The white settler population, which had been staunchly supportive of Ian Smith's government, was experiencing war fatigue. The economy was suffering under the weight of international sanctions, military expenditures, and the disruption of agriculture and industry caused by guerrilla attacks. The security situation in rural areas was increasingly precarious, with many white farmers becoming targets of guerrilla raids. The Rhodesian government attempted to bolster its military by conscripting more white settlers into the armed forces, but this move only fueled resentment among the population, many of whom had grown weary of the seemingly endless war.

By 1978, it had become clear to Ian Smith and his government that the war was unwinnable through military means alone. The combination of internal dissent, economic collapse, and the inability to defeat the guerrilla forces led to a shift in strategy. Smith, who had long vowed that there would be "no majority rule in Rhodesia, not in a thousand years," began to recognize that a political settlement was inevitable.

One of the first significant steps toward negotiations was the Internal Settlement Agreement, signed in March 1978. This agreement was an attempt by Smith to maintain white minority control while appeasing moderate African leaders who were willing to work with the government. The agreement created an interim government that included both white and black politicians, with the promise of eventual majority rule. Bishop Abel Muzorewa, a moderate African nationalist, became the first black prime minister under this arrangement.

However, the Internal Settlement failed to gain international recognition, and it did little to appease the more radical elements of the African nationalist movement. ZANU and ZAPU, which had continued their guerrilla campaigns, dismissed the settlement as a ploy by Smith to maintain white control. The Lancaster

House Agreement—a much more significant negotiation —was still on the horizon.

Throughout 1978 and 1979, the situation on the ground continued to deteriorate for the Rhodesian government. Guerrilla attacks increased, and the nationalist forces, particularly ZANLA, began to gain more control over rural areas. The war effort was increasingly unsustainable for Rhodesia, and Smith was left with few options other than to seek a comprehensive peace agreement.

The final push toward a negotiated settlement came in 1979, when the British government, under Prime Minister Margaret Thatcher, organized the Lancaster House Conference. This conference brought together representatives from the Rhodesian government, ZANU, ZAPU, and other African leaders to negotiate a peaceful transition to majority rule. The conference was held in London and was chaired by British Foreign Secretary Lord Carrington.

The negotiations were tense and difficult, with both sides making significant concessions. Ian Smith and the Rhodesian government reluctantly agreed to the principle of majority rule, while Mugabe and Nkomo agreed to respect property rights and the future role of the white minority in the new Zimbabwean government. The Lancaster House Agreement, signed in December 1979, paved the way for internationally supervised elections in 1980, which would lead to the creation of an independent Zimbabwe.

The elections, held in February 1980, were a decisive victory for Robert Mugabe and ZANU, who won a majority of the seats in the new parliament. On April 18, 1980, Zimbabwe officially gained independence and international recognition, with Mugabe becoming the country's first prime minister. The war was over, and the era of white minority rule in Rhodesia had come to an end.

The final years of the Rhodesian Bush War, from 1977 to 1979, were marked by a combination of military offensives like Operation Dingo and increasing political pressure both from within Rhodesia and from the international community. While the Rhodesian government achieved short-term military successes, it could not overcome the long-term strategic challenges posed by the guerrilla forces and international isolation. The war had become unsustainable, forcing Ian Smith to the negotiating table and ultimately leading to the end of white minority rule and the birth of Zimbabwe. This chapter highlights the complexities of the closing years of the war, as Rhodesia's military efforts were increasingly overshadowed by the inevitability of political change.

LANCASTER HOUSE AGREEMENT AND BIRTH OF ZIMBABWE

THE LANCASTER HOUSE AGREEMENT, SIGNED IN December 1979, marked the end of the Rhodesian Bush War and the beginning of a new era for Southern Africa. It was the result of months of intense negotiations between the Rhodesian government, led by Ian Smith, and the African nationalist movements, represented by Robert Mugabe of the Zimbabwe African National Union (ZANU) and Joshua Nkomo of the Zimbabwe African People's Union (ZAPU). The agreement, brokered by Britain, was a significant diplomatic achievement that paved the way for majority rule and the creation of Zimbabwe. This chapter explores the complex diplomatic process at Lancaster House, the key figures involved, and the compromises that were necessary to achieve peace.

The Lancaster House Conference was convened by the British government in September 1979. It was a last-ditch effort to end the protracted war and find a political solution to the conflict that had ravaged Rhodesia for nearly two decades. The conference took place at

Lancaster House in London and was chaired by British Foreign Secretary Lord Carrington, who played a critical role in facilitating the negotiations and ensuring that all parties remained engaged in the process.

The situation in Rhodesia had become increasingly untenable by the late 1970s. The guerrilla war waged by ZANLA (ZANU's military wing) and ZIPRA (ZAPU's military wing) had reached a stalemate, and the Rhodesian government, despite its superior military capabilities, could not suppress the nationalist movements. International pressure, especially from South Africa and the broader Commonwealth, had left Rhodesia isolated. Sanctions had taken a heavy toll on the Rhodesian economy, and the white settler population was growing weary of the war, fearing both for their security and their economic future.

The British government, under Prime Minister Margaret Thatcher, was keen to resolve the Rhodesian question, as it had become a significant issue in international diplomacy, particularly within the Commonwealth. Thatcher's administration recognized that majority rule was inevitable, but it also sought to protect the interests of the white minority in Rhodesia. Britain's role as the former colonial power meant it was well-positioned to mediate, but the stakes were high, as any agreement would have to satisfy both the Rhodesian government and the African nationalist movements.

Ian Smith, the long-time leader of Rhodesia, was a central figure at the Lancaster House Conference. For years, Smith had resisted any efforts to implement majority rule, famously declaring that there would be "no majority rule in Rhodesia, not in a thousand years." By 1979, Smith had come to the realization that the war could not be won militarily, and that some form of political compromise was necessary. Smith's main concern during the negotiations was to protect the interests of the white minority, particularly in terms of property rights and political representation in the new government.

Robert Mugabe, the leader of ZANU, emerged as the dominant figure on the African nationalist side. Mugabe had spent years leading the guerrilla war against the Rhodesian government, and by 1979, he was determined to achieve full majority rule. Mugabe's vision for Zimbabwe was rooted in Marxist principles, and he sought to dismantle the colonial structures that had kept the black majority disenfranchised. Despite his hardline rhetoric, Mugabe understood the importance of diplomacy and was willing to engage in the negotiations at Lancaster House to secure the end of white minority rule.

Joshua Nkomo, the leader of ZAPU, was another key figure in the talks. Nkomo had long advocated for a peaceful resolution to the conflict, but his forces had also played a significant role in the guerrilla war. Nkomo was seen as more moderate than Mugabe, and his vision for Zimbabwe included the possibility of power-sharing between different ethnic groups, particularly the Shona and Ndebele peoples.

The rivalry between Nkomo and Mugabe was a persistent undercurrent throughout the negotiations, as both men sought to position themselves as the future leader of Zimbabwe.

The Lancaster House negotiations were tense and complex, with both sides making significant compromises to reach an agreement. One of the most contentious issues was the question of land reform, which had been a central demand of the African nationalists. The white minority controlled the vast majority of Rhodesia's arable land, and the nationalists sought to redistribute this land to the black majority. However, the British government, along with the Rhodesian delegation, was concerned about the potential for economic collapse if land was confiscated without compensation. In the end, a compromise was reached: land reform would be delayed for at least ten years, and any redistribution would be carried out through a "willing buyer, willing seller" program, with funding from Britain and other international donors to compensate white landowners.

Another critical issue was the security and political rights of the white minority. The Rhodesian government, particularly Ian Smith, was adamant that the white population should retain a degree of political influence in the new Zimbabwe. The agreement included provisions for a two-house parliament, with reserved seats for the white minority in the upper house, ensuring that whites would have some representation, at least in the short term. Additionally, the Rhodesian Security Forces, including the military and police, would remain intact during the transition to majority rule, providing a degree of continuity and security for the white population.

On the other hand, the African nationalists, particularly Mugabe, were focused on achieving immediate majority rule and the dismantling of Rhodesia's apartheid-like system. The agreement guaranteed that elections would be held within months, and that the new government would be based on one-person, one-vote, effectively ending white minority rule. Mugabe and Nkomo both agreed to these terms, as they recognized that the war had reached a stalemate and that negotiations offered the best path to achieving independence.

The Lancaster House Agreement was signed on December 21, 1979, bringing an official end to the Rhodesian Bush War. The agreement laid out a framework for the transition to majority rule and established a timeline for free and fair elections, which would be monitored by the British government and international observers. The agreement also provided for a ceasefire, with both ZANLA and ZIPRA agreeing to lay down their arms and demobilize.

In February 1980, elections were held in Rhodesia, with Robert Mugabe and ZANU securing a decisive victory. Mugabe's party won fifty-seven out of eighty seats reserved for the black majority, while Nkomo's ZAPU won twenty seats. The white minority, represented by Ian Smith's Rhodesian Front, retained the twenty seats that had been set aside for whites. Despite concerns about potential violence and intimidation during the election, the process was largely peaceful, and the results were accepted by all parties.

On April 18, 1980, Rhodesia officially became Zimbabwe, with Robert Mugabe serving as the country's first Prime Minister. The transition from white minority rule to majority rule was completed, and the country embarked on a new chapter in its history. The Lancaster House Agreement had successfully ended the war, but it also set the stage for the challenges that Zimbabwe would face in the years to come, particularly regarding land reform, economic development, and national reconciliation.

The Lancaster House Agreement was a monumental achievement that ended the Rhodesian Bush War and brought about the birth of Zimbabwe. The negotiations at Lancaster House were marked by significant compromises, as both the Rhodesian government and the African nationalists had to make concessions to achieve peace. The agreement paved the way for majority rule and the creation of Zimbabwe, with Robert Mugabe emerging as the country's first leader. While the Lancaster House Agreement ended the conflict, it also left unresolved issues, particularly around land reform, that would continue to shape Zimbabwe's political landscape in the decades to come.

CONSEQUENCES AND LEGACY

The Rhodesian Bush War, also known as the Second Chimurenga, left an indelible mark on the political and social landscape of Zimbabwe and the broader Southern African region. While the conflict itself was a long and grueling struggle for control over Rhodesia's future, the consequences of the war had far-reaching implications that extended well beyond the borders of the newly formed Zimbabwe. The immediate and long-term effects of the war, its impact on regional stability, and the legacy of Robert Mugabe's leadership significantly shaped Zimbabwe's political and economic trajectory for decades.

Government statistics show that over 20,000 deaths occurred in the Rhodesian Bush War, including at least 468 white civilians and 7,790 black civilians.

It's hard to know accurate numbers because the Rhodesian Bush War was not an isolated conflict but rather a key event in the broader decolonization movement across Africa and parts of the war were fought outside of Rhodesian borders. By the late twentieth century, much of Africa had achieved independence from European colonial rule, but Southern Africa remained a bastion of white minority regimes, most notably in Rhodesia and apartheid-era South Africa. The successful resolution of the war, culminating in the Lancaster House Agreement and the establishment of Zimbabwe as an independent, majority-ruled state in 1980, represented a significant milestone in Africa's decolonization process.

One of the most immediate consequences of the war was further destabilization of the region, particularly in neighboring South Africa. The end of white minority rule in Rhodesia sent shockwaves through South Africa's apartheid regime, which had long viewed Rhodesia as a critical ally in its efforts to maintain racial segregation and white dominance. The fear among South African leaders was that the fall of Rhodesia would embolden anti-apartheid movements within their own country, particularly the African National Congress (ANC), which had close ties to Zimbabwe's nationalist forces.

Indeed, the liberation of Zimbabwe provided a significant boost to the anti-apartheid struggle. The victory of African nationalist forces in Zimbabwe demonstrated that even the most entrenched white minority regimes could be overthrown through a combination of armed struggle and international pressure. Zimbabwe, under Robert Mugabe's leadership, offered political and military support to the ANC, further strengthening the resolve of anti-apartheid activists within South Africa. While the apartheid regime would continue to resist change for another decade, the fall of Rhodesia was a clear sign that the days of white minority rule in South Africa were numbered.

In a broader sense, the Rhodesian Bush War also had a lasting impact on post-colonial Africa, particularly in terms of governance and the challenges of nation-building. Zimbabwe, like many newly independent African states, faced the daunting task of transitioning from a colonial economy and political system to one that reflected the needs and aspirations of the black majority. This process was fraught with difficulties, as the new government struggled to balance the expectations of its supporters with the realities of economic underdevelopment and the need to maintain stability in the face of lingering ethnic and political divisions.

When Robert Mugabe assumed leadership of Zimbabwe in 1980, he inherited a country that was still deeply divided along racial and political lines. On the one hand, the white minority, while no longer in political control, continued to dominate key sectors of the economy, particularly commercial farming, mining, and manufacturing. On the other hand, the black majority, many of whom had fought in the liberation war, expected significant changes in their economic and social conditions, particularly in terms of land ownership.

From the outset of his leadership, Mugabe faced the challenge of land reform, a central issue during the Rhodesian Bush War and a key demand of the African nationalist movements. During the Lancaster House negotiations, Mugabe had agreed to a "willing buyer, willing seller" land reform program, which aimed to redistribute land from white commercial farmers to landless black Zimbabweans. This program was slow to produce meaningful results, in part because the white minority, with international backing, remained reluctant to sell their land. For nearly two decades, land reform proceeded cautiously, with only a small percentage of Zimbabwe's prime agricultural land being transferred to black ownership.

However, by the late 1990s, land reform became a highly politicized and contentious issue. Mugabe, facing growing pressure from war veterans and political opponents, began to accelerate the process of land redistribution, often through extralegal means. In 2000, Mugabe's government launched the Fast Track Land Reform Program, which saw the seizure of white-owned farms, often by force, and their redistribution to black Zimbabweans. While this move was initially popular among Mugabe's supporters, it had disastrous consequences for Zimbabwe's economy.

The disruption of commercial farming, which had been the backbone of the country's economy, led to a sharp decline in agricultural production, food shortages, and economic collapse. The loss of experienced white farmers, combined with a lack of resources and training for the new landowners, crippled Zimbabwe's agricultural sector. This, in turn, led to hyperinflation, mass unemployment, and a humanitarian crisis, as the country struggled to feed its population. Zimbabwe's economy, once one of the most promising in Africa, entered a period of prolonged decline, from which it has yet to fully recover.

Mugabe's land policies, while rooted in the legitimate grievances of landless black Zimbabweans, became a symbol of the broader challenges facing post-colonial African states. The failure of land reform to deliver meaningful economic growth, combined with Mugabe's increasingly authoritarian rule, highlighted the difficulties of balancing revolutionary ideals with the practical realities of governance. Mugabe's legacy, once that of a liberation hero, became tarnished by the economic and political turmoil that followed his land reform efforts.

The Rhodesian Bush War and the subsequent transition to independence left a profound impact on Zimbabwe's political and economic trajectory. While the end of the war brought an end to white minority rule, it also ushered in a new set of challenges for the country, many of which continue to shape Zimbabwe's future.

Politically, the war and its aftermath solidified Robert Mugabe's dominance over the country. As the leader of the liberation struggle, Mugabe was able to consolidate power in the post-independence period, using his status as a war hero to silence opposition and maintain control over the government. Over time, Mugabe's rule became increasingly autocratic, with the ruling ZANU-PF party using state resources to suppress dissent and maintain its grip on power. The political landscape of Zimbabwe became characterized by a lack of democratic accountability, human rights abuses, and widespread corruption, all of which can be traced back to the legacy of the liberation war.

Economically, the disruption caused by the land reform program and the collapse of commercial agriculture had far-reaching consequences for Zimbabwe. The country, once a major exporter of food and agricultural products, became reliant on foreign aid and imports to meet its basic needs. The economic mismanagement of the Mugabe government, combined with international sanctions imposed in response to human rights abuses, further exacerbated the country's economic decline. Today, Zimbabwe continues to struggle with high levels of poverty, unemployment, and inflation, with many of its citizens seeking opportunities abroad due to the lack of economic prospects at home.

The social fabric of Zimbabwe was also deeply affected by the conflict and its aftermath. The war left behind deep scars, particularly in terms of ethnic and political divisions. The rivalry between ZANU and ZAPU, which had been a significant factor during the liberation struggle, continued to influence Zimbabwean politics in the post-independence period. Mugabe's government, dominated by the Shona ethnic group, often marginalized the Ndebele people, who had supported Nkomo's ZAPU during the war. This ethnic tension culminated in the Gukurahundi massacres of the 1980s, during which thousands of Ndebele civilians were killed by government forces in a brutal campaign to suppress opposition to Mugabe's rule.

The Rhodesian Bush War had far-reaching consequences for Zimbabwe and the broader region. While it ended white minority rule and paved the way for African self-determination, the war also set the stage for the economic and political challenges that would define Zimbabwe's post-colonial history. Robert Mugabe's leadership, initially celebrated as a victory for African nationalism, became increasingly associated with economic mismanagement, authoritarianism, and human rights abuses. The legacy of the war continues to shape Zimbabwe's political and economic landscape, as the country grapples with the difficult task of overcoming the divisions and challenges left in the wake of its liberation struggle.

Wrapping up our look at the Rhodesian Bush War, it's evident that this conflict was a key turning point in the wider fight for independence across Africa. The war, fought between 1964 and 1979, represented more than just a battle for control over Rhodesia—it was a microcosm of the wider decolonization movement that swept through Africa during the twentieth century. The complexities of this conflict, involving ethnic tensions, ideological divides, Cold War geopolitics, and deep-rooted historical grievances, provide important insights into the challenges of transitioning from colonial rule to independence.

At its core, the Rhodesian Bush War was a fight between white minority rule and African nationalism. For decades, Rhodesia had been ruled by a small white elite that controlled the country's political and economic systems, while the black majority was disenfranchised and marginalized. The nationalist movements—ZANU and ZAPU—rose up to challenge this inequitable system, demanding majority rule and independence. The war represented the culmination of years of frustration, as African communities sought to reclaim control over their own land and destiny.

The significance of the Rhodesian Bush War was part of a broader pattern of resistance to European colonialism across Africa. The eventual outcome of the war—the transition to majority rule in 1980—was a major victory for African nationalists and set an important precedent for other liberation movements in Southern Africa, particularly in Namibia and South Africa. The end of white minority rule in Rhodesia weakened the position of South Africa's apartheid regime and strengthened the resolve of anti-apartheid movements like the African National Congress (ANC), which would eventually bring about the end of apartheid laws in the early 1990s and the election of African nationalist Nelson Mandela as South Africa's first president.

The Rhodesian Bush War was also shaped by, and contributed to, the global dynamics of the Cold War. The involvement of the Soviet Union and China on the side of the nationalist forces and the clandestine support provided by South Africa and other Western-aligned powers to the Rhodesian government underscored the global stakes of the conflict. Rhodesia became a proxy battleground for competing ideologies: communism, as represented by the support for ZANU and ZAPU, and capitalism, embodied by the white settler government's desire to maintain its economic system.

In this sense, the Rhodesian Bush War offers a case study of the complexities of guerrilla warfare and how asymmetric conflicts can shape the trajectory of national liberation movements. The success of the nationalist forces, despite the Rhodesian military's tactical prowess, demonstrated that guerrilla warfare could be an effective means of resistance against more established and better-equipped regimes. The war highlighted the importance of securing local support, exploiting international backing, and using unconventional tactics to overcome superior firepower.

The Lancaster House Agreement of 1979 marked the end of the conflict, paving the way for the birth of Zimbabwe in 1980. This was a monumental achievement, but it also set the stage for the challenges that

Zimbabwe would face as it transitioned from colonial rule to independence. The war had left deep scars on the country, not just in terms of physical destruction, but also in the form of ethnic and political divisions, economic underdevelopment, and unresolved land ownership issues.

The Bush War teaches us important lessons about the dynamics of decolonization, the use of guerrilla warfare in achieving political objectives, and the challenges of post-colonial governance. One of the key takeaways from the conflict is the difficulty of balancing revolutionary ideals with the practical realities of state-building. While the end of white minority rule was a significant victory for African nationalism, it did not immediately translate into economic prosperity, political stability, or equality among ethnicities with the black majority. The legacies of colonialism, including entrenched inequalities and external economic dependencies, continued to shape Zimbabwe's post-independence future.

Another lesson from the Bush War is the importance of diplomatic negotiations in ending protracted conflicts. The Lancaster House Agreement, while imperfect, provided a framework for a peaceful transition to majority rule. It demonstrated that even deeply entrenched conflicts can be resolved through negotiation and compromise, as long as all parties are willing to engage in dialogue.

The Bush War left behind a complicated legacy—one that would continue to shape Zimbabwe's political, social, and economic development for decades to come.

As we look back on this war, it is important to recognize its place within the broader history of African independence movements. The war serves as a reminder of the complexities of decolonization, the difficult choices faced by liberation movements, and the lasting consequences of conflict in newly independent states. Zimbabwe's journey from colonial rule to independence is a story of both triumph and tragedy, and the lessons of that journey continue to resonate across the African continent and beyond.

Enter into a World of Warfare History

Go to wrinnmilitaryhistory.com and get your free book **WW2: Spies, Snipers and Tales of the World at War**. I'll also add you to my military history readers group where I occasionally send out emails with details on new releases and special offers.

BIBLIOGRAPHY

Blake, Robert. *A History of Rhodesia*. Eyre Methuen, 1977.
A foundational account of Rhodesia's history, offering essential context from colonialism to the rise of African nationalism and the war.
Cilliers, Jakkie. *Counter-Insurgency in Rhodesia*. Croom Helm, 1985.
An in-depth analysis of Rhodesia's counter-insurgency strategies, including key military operations and tactics used during the war.
Godwin, Peter, and Ian Hancock. *Rhodesians Never Die: The Impact of War and Political Change on White Rhodesia, c. 1970–1980*. Oxford University Press, 1993.
A sociopolitical analysis of how the Bush War affected the white settler population and their perceptions of the conflict.
Martin, David, and Phyllis Johnson. *The Struggle for Zimbabwe: The Chimurenga War*. Faber and Faber, 1981.
A comprehensive overview of the liberation struggle, focusing on the political and military dimensions of the conflict.
Moorcraft, Paul L., and Peter McLaughlin. *The Rhodesian War: A Military History*. Jonathan Ball, 2008.
A detailed military history of the war, examining key battles, strategies, and the role of the Rhodesian armed forces.
Noir, René. "The Fall of Rhodesia." *Popular Social Science*, October 29, 2020. https://www.popularsocialscience.com/the-fall-of-rhodesia/.
An accessible analysis of Rhodesia's decline, focusing on the political, economic, and social factors that contributed to its eventual collapse.
Smith, Ian. *The Great Betrayal: The Memoirs of Ian Douglas Smith*. Blake Publishing, 1997.
The personal account of Rhodesia's leader during the war, offering insight into his perspective on the conflict and the UDI.
Stedman, Stephen John. *Peacemaking in Civil War: International Mediation in Zimbabwe, 1974–1980*. Lynne Rienner Publishers, 1991.
A study of the diplomatic efforts, including the Lancaster House Agreement, that ultimately brought an end to the Rhodesian Bush War.
Stedman, Stephen John. *Peacemaking in Civil War: International Mediation in Zimbabwe, 1974–1980*. Lynne Rienner Publishers, 1991.
A study of the diplomatic efforts, including the Lancaster House Agreement, that ultimately brought an end to the Rhodesian Bush War.

Mongoose Bravo: Vietnam: A Time of Reflection Over Events So Long Ago

"A frank, real, memoir" – Reviewer

Uncover the gritty, real-life story of a Vietnam combat veteran.

With an engaging and authentic retelling of his experiences as an infantry soldier of the B Co., 1/5th 1st Cavalry Division in the Vietnam War, this gripping account details the life and struggles of war in a strange and foreign country.

What started as a way of bringing closure to a grieving mother morphed into a memoir, covering the author's deployment, duty, and eventual return to the United States after the end of the war. Imbued with the emotion that he felt during this conflicted time, along with letters and journal entries from decades ago, this memoir is a testament to the sacrifice that these brave men and women made fighting on foreign soil.

Recounting the tragedies of war and the chaos of combat as an infantry soldier, in the words of the author: "We lived, and fought as a unit, covering each other's backs. Most came home to tell their own stories, many didn't."

If you like gripping, authentic accounts of life and combat during the Vietnam War, then you won't want to miss Mongoose Bravo: Vietnam: A Time of Reflection Over Events So Long Ago.

WORLD WAR II PACIFIC: BATTLES AND CAMPAIGNS FROM GUADALCANAL TO OKINAWA 1942-1945

"A brisk and compelling game changer for the historiography of the Pacific Theater in World War II." – Reviewer

An enlightening glimpse into nine battles and campaigns during the Pacific War Allied offensive.

Each of these momentous operations were fascinating feats of strategy, planning, and bravery, handing the Allies what would eventually become a victory over the Pacific Theater and an end to Imperialist Japanese expansion.

Operation Watchtower, a riveting exploration of the spark that set off the Allied offensive in the Pacific islands, detailing the grueling struggle for the island of Guadalcanal and its vital strategic position.

Operation Galvanic, an incredible account of the battle for the Tarawa Atoll and base that would give them a steppingstone into the heart of Japanese-controlled waters.

Operation Backhander, a gripping retelling of the war for Cape Gloucester, New Guinea, and the Bismarck Sea.

Battle for Saipan, Marines stormed the beaches with a goal of gaining a crucial air base from which the US could launch its new long-range B-29 bombers directly at Japan's home islands.

Invasion of Tinian, is the incredible account of the assault on Tinian. Located just under six miles southwest of Saipan. This was the first use of napalm and the "shore to shore" concept.

Recapture of Guam, a gripping narrative about the liberation of the Japanese-held island of Guam, captured by the Japanese in 1941 during one of the first Pacific campaigns of the War.

Operation Stalemate, Marines landed on the island of Peleliu, one of the Palau Islands in the Pacific, as part of a larger operation to provide support for General MacArthur, who was preparing to invade the Philippines.

Operation Detachment, the battle of Iwo Jima was a major offensive in World War II. The Marine invasion was tasked with the mission of capturing airfields on the island for use by P-51 fighters.

Operation Iceberg, the invasion and ultimate victory on Okinawa was the largest amphibious assault in the Pacific Theater. It was also one of the bloodiest battles in the Pacific, lasting ninety-eight days.

This gripping narrative sheds light on these often-overlooked facets of WWII, providing students, history fans, and World War II buffs alike with a captivating breakdown of the history and combat that defined the ultimate victory of US forces in the Pacific.

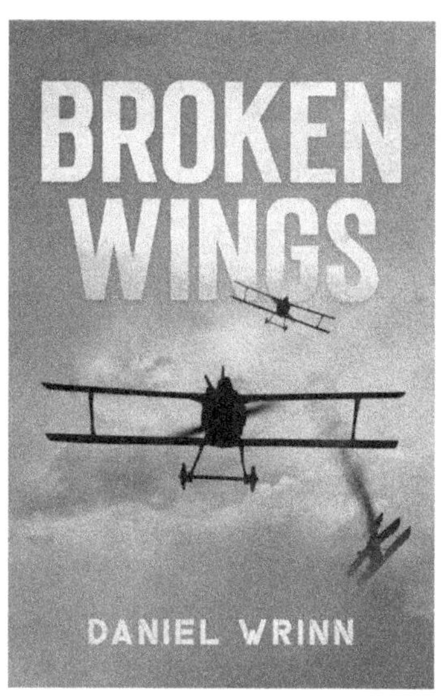

Broken Wings: WWI Fighter Ace's Story of Escape and Survival

"A masterfully told story of triumph and redemption in a powerfully drawn survival epic." – Reviewer

Hero WWI Fighter Pilot Shot Down and Captured.

With an engaging and authentic retelling of his experiences as an escaped prisoner of war, this gripping account details the life and struggles of a captured pilot in 1917 war-torn Europe.

Lieutenant John Ryan couldn't wait to see action in WWI. He joined up with the British colors out of Canada. As one of several American pilots in the Royal Flying Corps before the US joined the war, he earned his wings and became an Ace through fierce air battles over the skies of Germany.

www.ingramcontent.com/pod-product-compliance
Lightning Source LLC
Chambersburg PA
CBHW051352150726
48000CB00003B/1145